I CAN'T FIX YOU— BECAUSE YOU'RE NOT BROKEN

The Eight Keys to Freeing Yourself from Painful Thoughts and Feelings

Jo Eckler, Psy.D., RYT

Spiral Staircase Publishing

Austin, Texas

Jo Eckler/Spiral Staircase Publishing
Austin, TX 78704
www.spiralstaircasepublishing.com

Publisher's Note: This work is not a substitute for professional psychotherapy or other mental health treatment.

Book Layout © 2017 BookDesignTemplates.com

Book Cover created by Sage House Marketing and Design, © 2018 Jo Eckler

Author Photo by Erica Nix, © 2015 Jo Eckler

I can't fix you--Because you're not broken: The eight keys to freeing yourself from painful thoughts and feelings. -- 1st ed.
ISBN 978-0-692-10165-0

For all those who have been brave enough to share their stories with me.

CONTENTS

Of Toasters and Humans

You are not a toaster. At least, if you are reading this, I am assuming you're not a toaster. I know appliances are getting smarter every day with technology, but I'm guessing they're still a long way from picking up self-help books.

Now that we've established that you're (most likely) not a toaster, here's why that matters. You're not a toaster because you can't break. Appliances break, windows break, KitKat bars break, coffee breaks (wheee! Puns!), but people don't break.

"But Dr. Jo," you say. "I feel so broken! I feel damaged and shattered and deficient. I feel like there is something inherently wrong with me, and if anyone ever found out what it was, they would despise me."

You feel how you feel—I will never argue about what emotions you may be experiencing at any given time. All emotions are valid. Even those that aren't attached to reality.

However, here's the deal. Although you may feel broken and like every cell in your body is screaming that it's true, you're not actually broken.

Read that through a few more times. That's right: you're not actually broken. You don't have to believe it yet, or ever. I just ask that you give me the rest of this book before you decide.

By the way, you might notice that I use "we" an awful lot in this book. I do that on purpose. I'm writing about common human experience, so it's likely that I've been there, that you've been there, and that your roommate who picks up this book when you leave it in the bathroom and their smartphone battery has died has been there. Hence, "we."

Because we're all in this, together.

CHAPTER ONE

Why We're Having This Conversation

Sometimes people look at the word "psychologist" in my title and decide that I have somehow bypassed pain, sorrow, and anxiety and have a completely put-together life. That my floors are spotless, my checkbook balanced, and my mind a sunshiny meadow swept by sweet breezes that smell faintly of lavender. This gets even worse when they see "yoga teacher" and they start adding on a perfectly balanced diet of dark leafy greens and sustainably harvested nuts between my hours of daily yoga and blissful meditation practice.

What a load of B.S. I can't speak for all mental health professionals and yoga teachers, but I came to this work—was pushed into this work—by life events that ambushed me, overwhelmed my emotional and mental defenses, and mugged me in dark alleys.

And oh, boy howdy did they take me down. Way down. Like making deals with myself that if things didn't improve in the next five years that I would kill myself down. I'll spare you the whole list. Suffice it to say that I renewed that deal with myself twice between the ages of 15 and 25. Things did-n't get a whole lot easier after age 25, but I felt more able to hang in there.

I tried so many things to make those awful feelings go away. I poured alcohol, cigarettes, ice cream, and pizza into that emptiness inside, hoping to fill the void for even a moment. I tracked my thoughts. I recited affirmations. I walked. I listened to happy music. I tried to look on the bright side of life. I checked out armfuls of self-help books from the library. I got a degree. Then a doctorate. I moved to other cities, other states. I broke off romances, bounced into new beds. I binged on French films, on marathons of reality shows. I read *The Bell Jar* and *Prozac Nation* and cried in recognition (when I wasn't beating myself up for being so unhappy when I had so much going for me).

Gradually other things crept into my awareness, like the concept of mindfulness. I was lucky enough to be able to access training and books through my job as a psychologist that let me explore mindfulness, which was a gateway to yoga, which was a door to other forms of being present and sitting with the tough stuff that life kicks up.

Along with all of those things, I owe immense gratitude to Acceptance and Commitment Therapy, which has the fun acronym ACT (pronounced like the verb "to act"). I took a training about ACT right before one of my dear coworkers was killed in an automobile accident while on the way to work, and it gave me the tools to navigate through that and its aftermath without completely falling apart. I continue to lean on these principles day after day both personally and in my work with my clients. My offerings to you here are deeply infused with the principles of ACT, so if you like them, I encourage you to seek out a therapist trained in ACT or some of the other wonderful self-help books based in ACT. I owe immense gratitude to all who have worked to develop this therapy and who have trained me, especially Steven Hayes and Robyn Walsh. You can learn more and access a directory of ACT practitioners at https://contextualscience.org/

We're having this conversation because I know you've been suffering. I know that you're getting tired of trying everything you can to make the pain stop, striving to get to some kind of peace in your life. I know that it can feel so scary to be in the world when everyone else seems to have it together and yet the seemingly smallest thing can launch a panic attack or a flashback or a paralyzing barrage of self-loathing and shame. I know staying at home, staying in bed, staying small gets really boring—and yet to try anything else can feel terrifying. I know sometimes you lose hope, and sometimes you don't dare hope for fear of being disappointed.

Dear, dear one, please hang on a little longer. Read this book. Try it on. I can't make anything go away, but I want to offer you what I've found that has helped me and many others be able to take the steps to start living, not just dragging ourselves from hour to hour. It's not going to be quick and easy, but it'll be worth it.

CHAPTER TWO

How to Use This Book

This book is meant to be a brief field manual. Each chapter is short, but there's a lot to explore in each one. As you travel through the pages, you'll find opportunities to make the concepts more relevant to your own internal and external life. There are exercises, suggestions, and other helpful resources.

I want you to take a week with each chapter. The exercises are most beneficial if you try them multiple times over the course of a week rather than just one time on one day. Remember, practice is essential to master these keys sufficiently to prepare you to use them even when in distress. If you want to get really fancy, sit down once a week at the same day and time and pretend it's your weekly session with me. Make yourself space to do this work.

To help keep you accountable, pick a person you trust and let them know you're working on weekly assignments. You don't even have to tell them exactly what you're working on. Ask if you can check in with them to let them know when you finish an assignment or if you need encouragement to do an assignment. This can be done over text, email, phone, in person—whatever works for you and your support person.

Speaking of support, this book can be used in conjunction with any other therapy, healing, or personal growth work you might be doing. If you don't have a therapist, you might consider one, especially if you have a history of traumatic experience. And please, if you're having serious thoughts about hurting yourself or someone else, contact 911, go to your nearest emergency room, or call the crisis hotline at 1-877-223-SAFE.

I recommend going through the whole book in order once, then later returning to any chapter as needed for review and reminders. I have certain books that I keep handy even though I've read them multiple times. Now and then I pick one up and open it to a random page to get a little reminder and encouragement. This book would work well for that too, so hang onto it. It'll be here when you need it.

Chapter Three

The Governor (A Few Words about the Process of Change)

Before we dive into the Eight Keys, it would be helpful to say a few words about the process of making changes in our lives. Clearly, it's hard stuff, because otherwise you'd have done more of it already. Even a simple change can have many layers.

There's this thing that is put on car engines called a governor. It's designed to keep the engine from being able to go as fast as it is actually able, used for safety reasons and also to give law enforcement a head start.

We often have our own version of a governor. In an abusive relationship, whether it is with a romantic partner, a parent, a work supervisor, a friend group, or a teacher, the mechanism is very clear (at least in hindsight; it's harder to see it when we're in it). It can start as discouragement, like them saying "why don't you skip pottery class tonight and come cuddle with me?" In some cases, it shows up as criticism, insults, or even physical, social, or financial violence when we engage in an activity. Perhaps the abuser has a crisis every time we're scheduled to give an important presentation at work, to go to a training, or take a trip with friends. In response, we postpone, cancel, change our plans. It can naturally follow to quit the team, stop vying for that promotion, or forget to go to our volunteer shift. It all can fall away without us even noticing, especially if great affection is poured upon us for staying in, for staying small.

This phenomenon can also happen through a gradual chipping away of our confidence. We might be told that we're no good at sports anyway. Maybe we hear them say that our coworkers are smarter and we'll never get anywhere at that job. Or they question how we can expect to succeed at our art if we can't even make coffee right. If we're isolated from those who see our gifts and believe in us, we start believing that we're no good, and we might stop trying.

Then there's outright punishment. The ultimate governor. And very hard to forget, whether it be physical, emotional, financial, or social.

Our mind is geared towards safety, and it firmly believes that it's better to be safe than sorry. Hence, we can internalize that governor. We can punish ourselves before we get punished, discourage ourselves before someone else can do it. If we can beat them to the punch (sometimes literally), it seems to hurt a little less. It gives us a sense of control in a helpless situation. We can become so adept at this that we continue it years or decades after the relationship or situation ends.

Why? Because we're designed for safety, not comfort. To do something different, to stretch and move outside the familiar, is to put ourselves at risk. It is dangerous. If not physically dangerous, it may be emotionally dangerous. This inherent tendency is compounded when we have been "taught" through an abusive relationship that to change or grow is to suffer painful consequences.

There are so many types of governors. Procrastination, for starters. Overwork in one area that allows us to neglect our physical health. Starting but not following through. Finding people who are happy to take up all of our time and attention so that we can't possibly start that enterprise or write that opera because they need us. That voice inside that calls us selfish and greedy, uncaring and rude, for wanting to do our own thing. Voices that say it'll never work, why bother, others have done it better, it's all been done before. Avoidance—of checkbooks, of making that call, of taking that class. Sometimes our bodies even get in on the fun and start causing trouble at the first signs of serious change. So many ways to stay small!

Even if we make it out of whatever abusive or invalidating situation we are in and start to disregard our own governors, there's one more test: the world. There are people in our lives who may feel nervous and threatened if we start to do something new or different. Maybe the relationship was founded upon us giving and them taking. Maybe our brave steps stir up their own insecurities and regrets about not taking brave steps themselves. Perhaps we befriended them at a time when we were convinced that small was the only option, and the relationship no longer fits the expanded version of us. Those voices we heard inside our heads will move into the people around us, and we'll face the challenge of talking back to them and doing what we want to do anyway.

That right there? That's when we've really claimed our power. When we can hear the naysaying voices and do it anyway. Once we've mastered that, we're pretty darn unstoppable.

EXPLORATIONS

What feels scary for you about the possibility of feeling more engaged and alive?

What intrigues you about it?

Before continuing your journey into this book, create a reminder for yourself of why you want to do this work in the first place. What's important to you about learning new ways to relate to your thoughts and feelings? The reminder you create can be visual (like collage, drawing, or photographs), a letter to yourself, or even a song. You don't have to share it with anyone, but just make sure you can keep it somewhere where it will remind you of why you chose to open this book.

Chapter Four

Key One: Noticing

Now the moment we've been preparing for! The first key! It's Noticing. Yeah, I know, it doesn't sound like much. But it's the key to the keys. It's the one that will help us use all the other keys. We might even say that it's the key to unlock the keys.

When dealing with our minds, it helps to develop the skill of noticing. Noticing our thought patterns, noticing shifts in our body, noticing whatever is actually happening in this moment.

Noticing has many names. Here I'll use it interchangeably with mindfulness, meaning, as Jon Kabut-Zinn says, "paying attention, to one thing, on purpose, in the moment, non-judgmentally." The thing we select as the target of our focus can be anything at all, internal or external. The quality of our attention is what's important here. It's an openness and curiosity about whatever we may find rather than expectations and assumptions of what we will find.

There's a phrase I give to almost all of my clients that comes, like many of these concepts, from Acceptance and Commitment Therapy (ACT). It's to be practiced on a regular basis, at least a few times a day, with any kind of thought or sensation. As when learning anything, it's best to start with easy steps, so use neutral or less painful thoughts or sensations at first rather than the heavy stuff.

Ready? Here's the magic mantra (not really magic, but the alliteration is irresistible):

I'm noticing I'm having the thought that ___(insert thought here)

Other variations are:

I'm noticing I'm having the sensation of _____.

I'm noticing I'm having the feeling/emotion of _____.

What goes in that blank is the most objective description that can be mustered for that thought/sensation/feeling. That's important here.

Let's break this down a little more to see why this is the magic mantra.

I'm noticing. This phrase instantly gives us a little space from our mind, brings us back to ourselves. There is an "I" and that "I" is actively doing something. That "I" is being mindful.

I'm having. Here we remind ourselves that we are having the thought—the thought isn't having us. This puts us back in the driver's seat.

The thought that ___. Naming is powerful. When we can name a thought or feeling, it gives us a way to relate to it. This also puts the thought in its place. The beginning parts of the phrase reminded us to be mindful and that we're in control, and this third part helps us see exactly what it is that we're in control of in this moment. Here we remind ourselves that it is a thought we are dealing with and not a reality.

What's with all these parts? Our mind is a strange beast because we can think about thinking. This is getting pretty meta, I know. The part of us that can think about thinking is what I call The Noticer. In some traditions or belief systems, this might be known as the soul, spirit, wise mind, true self, higher self, observer, recorder, and so on. It's the part of us that has been watching and recording memories and experiences our entire lives.

Here's another thing about the Noticer—it is indestructible. No matter what we do or how intense an experience has been, the Noticer has been there the whole time. Our entire lives. Watching, but unaffected, like it's behind a protected force field. We can think back on a memory from our younger years and almost watch our little selves like a movie, all thanks to the Noticer.

When we strengthen the Noticer, we strengthen our ability to make choices rather than impulsively react. So give it a try, remembering that it takes many repetitions to create a habit of any kind, including a mental one.

EXPLORATIONS

Have you ever experienced being the Noticer? What activities or situations help you shift into that perspective?

There are many ways to strengthen our noticing muscle. Pick one of these short and sweet mindfulness techniques to try each day for a week:

Forget How to Do Something: Pretend that you've forgotten how to do something that you usually do every day, like brush your teeth or make your breakfast. When you do that task, do it with as much attention as you would if you were doing it for the first time. What muscles do you use? What smells or sounds do you notice? Whenever your mind wanders, bring yourself back to the task at hand and your senses.

Three Slow-Motion Bites: This is best done at the beginning or end of a meal, although you can throw them in at any point. Slow down as you approach your food. Take a look at it, noticing colors, textures, how it catches the light. Smell it. Check in with your body and how it is starting to respond to looking at the food. The mind will probably chime in too, and you can just notice those thoughts as part of the experience. As you take your first bite, really pay attention to the temperature, texture, and flavors that start to emerge. Chew slowly, following the flavors as they shift and change. Wait a second or two longer than you usually would before swallowing, then pay attention to the food as it travels down to your stomach. Give yourself a moment to notice the flavors left in your mouth, then slowly repeat the process with the next two bites.

What's New? This one is great on a busy day. Each time you go into or out of a place that you visit often (this can also include rooms in your house), look for something that you've never noticed before. It can be anything.

Find a Focus: **Pick** one thing to focus on. Some ideas are a piece of music, a picture, a candle, looking out the window, your breath, or a phrase or mantra. Sit comfortably and let your spine be long to let your mind know that it needs to pay attention. Set a timer of some kind—three minutes is a good starting point. Direct your attention to the thing you chose to focus on. Each time you notice that your mind wanders off somewhere else, gently bring it back to your chosen focus point. Repeat as many times as needed, as often as needed, until the timer dings. (No matter how often you get distracted, you're still strengthening the muscle of your attention, so you can't fail at this as long as you actually do the exercise.)

Want more practice? There are gazillions of books, audio recordings, videos, smartphone apps, and classes on mindfulness out there. Some are connected with spirituality or religious paths, but many have no such connections. With so many to choose from, if you don't like the first one you find, you can keep trying until you land on one that fits your style.

The key to the door of mindfulness is to practice on a regular basis, even if it is for a very short time. I like to get a pack of stickers or gold stars and put them on my wall calendar to mark each day I do my practice. It's encouraging to see the stickers cover the calendar. (Plus, I really like stickers.) Think about what might work for you as a tracking and reward system.

CHAPTER FIVE

Key Two: There's More Room than You Realize

So now that you know about the indestructible Noticer, there's another layer we can add. Let's call this one Zoom. It's a fitting name, since this key allows us to shift perspective in such a way that we are better able to withstand anything that comes our way.

This metaphor from ACT can help here. If you know something about the game of chess, you know it's played on a board with alternating black and white squares. One player has black pieces; the other has white ones. The game is played by moving pieces according to certain rules to eliminate the other player's pieces from the board. In this example, let's say that the board is infinitely large, stretching out forever in every direction.

For the pieces, chess is a battle to the death. Each time a piece meets another, one of them has to "die" (be removed from the board). There is no negotiation or room for compromise. It's serious business at this level.

This piece level is where we often spend much of our time. We can pit a "positive affirmation" white piece against a "negative thought" black piece. A "think happy thoughts" white one against a "traumatic memory" black one. New pieces are being added to the board all the time as we have more thoughts and experiences, making this an exhausting battle to maintain. Remember, for the pieces it's a battle to the death, which is based in the belief that the other piece will destroy us.

There's another option. What if we live at the level of the board? The infinitely large board? In chess, the pieces may "die," but the board remains. It cannot be damaged in the fight. It has plenty of room for all the pieces that are already there, as well as for all the pieces that will come in the future. The board is not in a life-or-death battle. It simply observes. Sure, it might shake a little or the battles might get noisy, but the board remains intact.

Can you feel that in your body for just a moment? That expansiveness, that spaciousness? Maybe you feel it in your chest, the breath coming just a little more easily. Or your shoulders drop down and back slightly. The jaw softens.

When we're feeling caught in a struggle, whether it's with a thought, a physical sensation, or being generally overwhelmed, that's seeing things from the level of the pieces. Once we recognize that, we can zoom out to the board level, giving us perspective and some comfort that this one thing is not all we are and that we can survive it. In fact, the board gives us vivid evidence of how many other thoughts, emotions, memories, and experiences we have survived before. Which is ALL of them. We have a 100% survival rate of all the things we have ever experienced. (Unless you're reading this book from some sort of afterlife, in which case, say hi to my deceased friends and family for me. That's highly unlikely, so let's stick with the 100% survival rate).

Another way to think of this concept is to imagine ourselves as the sky. Even though storms and clouds and birds and planes and Superman and hot air balloons move through the sky, it's still the sky. It remains essentially unchanged, and it has room for all of that stuff and more.

What would be different if we moved through our lives, or even a day, believing that we have enough space for whatever thoughts, sensations, emotions, and experiences may come? What's more, what if we believed that NONE OF IT COULD DESTROY US?

What would we stop hiding from? What would we be able to do? How would we face challenges? What habits would fall away? How would it change how we interact with others?

We often say things like "I can't take one more thing." The thing is, we can. And we always have.

EXPLORATIONS

When have you been at the piece level? What did it feel like?

When have you been at the board level? How did you know? How did it feel?

What helps you shift to the board level? What can pull you down to piece level before you know it?

Practice Zooming (changing perspective from piece level to board level) each day. You might imagine it like a movie camera zooming in for the close-up, then panning out for the wide sweeping shot. In fact, start paying attention to how cameras zoom in and out when you're watching TV or movies. How does it change how you feel about the scene?

Come up with a phrase to serve as a reminder to yourself to zoom out. It can be anything, as long as you know what it means, like "zoom out" or "change levels." Then create something visual that can remind you to remind yourself to zoom out.

CHAPTER SIX

Key Three: You Don't Have to Do Everything Your Mind Says

Now that we have the keys of Noticing and Zoom in hand, we can move into the third key: Thanks But No Thanks. This name will make more sense soon; just know that this key can give you more freedom of movement in your choices as you go through your day. For some of my clients, this was the only thing they needed to hear—it made that much of a change for them.

This was a toughie to wrap my mind around at first (pun intended—these are the jokes, folks!). I've spent decades and large sums of money on my mind, filling it with information and training it to do some nice party tricks. I've been an academic overachiever and incessant reader. My mind was the place to be, at least for me. Since my body hasn't been very cooperative over the years, my mind rose to even greater importance.

Our mind is really good at solving problems. It can perform mathematical computations, keep a running tally of how much toilet paper we have, design a chair, create a new language. It can help us figure out how to buy grapes or go to Australia. This is awesome!

We run into problems when our mind tries to use the same tools that it uses to solve problems outside of ourselves to address problems inside of ourselves. It's like using a hammer for every task; it's just not the right tool.

The other issue with this approach is that our internal feelings, sensations, and thoughts are not problems. Read that over a few more times and let it sink in.

Emotions and other internal experiences are not the problem. They are going to happen no matter what—they're a part of being human. They're part of our survival wiring. They are not always comfortable, but they aren't dangerous.

Whoa there, Dr. Jo! Hold up! What about people who commit suicide because they're so depressed or who do something violent because they're angry? Aren't emotions dangerous?

Let's take this apart a little. It's not the emotion itself that did those things. An emotion is not going to automatically push you off a roof. Emotions don't have arms, for one. There are some intermediate steps involved:

Step 1: The emotion arises (could also be a physical sensation like pain, a mental experience like a hallucination, or a pattern of thoughts).

Step 2: Our mind starts telling us a story about what that emotion means, how long it will stick around, what it means about us that we're having the emotion, our ability to withstand the emotion, what we need to do to change the emotion, etc. Our minds have a LOT to say about this topic!

Step 3: WE BELIEVE WHAT OUR MIND IS SAYING.

Step 4: We take action based on that belief in what our mind is saying.

Step 5: Repeat.

Here's an example. Let's say we start noticing a slight headache in the front of our head. This is what could ensue:

Step 1: Dull, aching pain begins in the front of our head.

Step 2: Mind says: "Uh oh, we're getting a headache. Probably going to turn into a migraine and we'll be stuck in bed the rest of the day. Perfect timing—that big event is tonight and now we're not going to get to go. They're going to be so mad at us and not invite us to anything anymore, and we'll have no friends. We're going to die alone. We could have met the love of our lives tonight and now we'll never know. And of course, now we're going to have to call into work tomorrow because we're sure that this is going to get worse so we'll lose out on that income and the boss could fire us. We're going to die poor and alone and eaten by wild dogs since we'll get evicted too. Wait, what if it's a brain tumor? There was that article that other day...probably be a good idea to look this up on the internet...."

Step 3: WE BELIEVE WHAT OUR MIND IS SAYING. We become the mind's "yes person," nodding and bowing and saying, "yes, yes, Mind, you're totally right, whatever you think is best, yes Mind, right away."

Step 4: We take action. Initiate frantic internet search. Agree with mind that it is definitely a tumor. Head to local urgent care clinic to get confirmation. Write letters in the waiting room to everyone we know expressing apologies and love since we're sure we'll be dead in six months from the tumor. Spend the next six hours and a lot of money learning that it is likely a sinus headache (that in fact is already fading).

Miss event due to choosing to go to the clinic. Lose income due to deciding to go to the clinic. Very tired for work the next day.

(Please consult with a physician about any new or unusual medical symptoms! I'm not trying to discourage you from doing that. This is an extreme example for educational purposes.)

Here's another example using depression:

Step 1: We start to experience feelings of sadness and heaviness.

Step 2: Mind chimes in with: "Oh no, here we go again, another major depressive episode. The last one was so awful—we almost didn't make it through that. We can't handle this again. It's too much. If we were better or stronger, maybe we could, but we're too weak. Other people seem to do it just fine, so there must be something really wrong with us that we're in this much pain. This is never going to end, it's just going to keep getting worse. There's nothing we can do about it. Everyone would hate us if they knew how awful we feel. It's so hard to do anything right now, why even bother? What's the point? Better to just stay in bed. They'd be better off without us anyway."

Step 3: WE BELIEVE WHAT OUR MIND IS SAYING. "Yes Mind, you know best, Mind, what you say must be true."

Step 4: We take action. Ignoring phone calls or texts. Stay in bed. Skip the shower. Skip eating (or eat everything we can find). Put off the tasks on the to-do list. Miss a birthday party. Snap at our roommate or partner. Pull the covers over our head and watch 20 hours of a TV show that we don't even particularly like.

Step 5: Our mind uses our actions as more evidence in the case against us, and we believe it more and more, giving rise to feelings of worthlessness, helplessness, and hopelessness. This can continue to spiral downward until something breaks the cycle.

This is a process that happens for all of us. It can happen with any kind of internal experience, comfortable or uncomfortable, including memories. It will continue to happen. There is a key point where we can create shifts, however. Traditionally, therapy and self-help has focused on Step 2 and tried to change what the mind says, using affirmations, thought records, arguing with our thoughts, trying to stop "negative" thoughts, and so on, with varying levels of success. Some approaches have looked at Step 4, targeting behavior change as a way to impact emotions, which has been helpful to some degree but can be very difficult in the midst of deep depression or intense anxiety.

Step 3 is the turning point. The actions we choose to take in Step 4 are directly related to our decision to believe what the mind says.

Here's what's different about this approach. We don't have to get the mind to be quiet. We don't have to argue with it or change what it says. We don't have to do anything except stop believing what it says.

This may seem easier said than done, but there are probably plenty of times that you have heard or seen something and not believed it. Think of all the sales pitches, spam emails, infomercials, commercials, billboards, slick magazine ads, package labels, and junk mail we get. Maybe at first we get sucked into believing that we really do need that shiny new gadget or that it'll be such a good deal to buy this thing. But over time, we get used to the marketing banter and tune out most of it. It becomes background noise, our attention returning once a new song starts or our show resumes. We learn to distinguish what is likely to be useful from what is just hype.

This is the same process we can use for filtering through the messages from our mind. Our mind is an organ, like the stomach. The stomach makes acid, the brain makes thoughts. Sweat glands make sweat, the brain makes thoughts. That's its job. There is nothing in the brain's job description saying that these thoughts have to be useful, make sense, or be true. It just has to keep making them. I often visualize this as either the ticker that runs across the bottom of 24-hour news channels displaying headlines, or as Lucille Ball in the scene from *I Love Lucy* where she is desperately trying to keep up with an assembly line of chocolates. If we try to analyze and control all of our thoughts, we'll end up like Lucy: exhausted, frantic, and hopelessly behind. (And possibly covered in chocolate.)

Viewing the mind in this way can help us get a little space from it. This wiggle room allows us to make choices instead of simply reacting to everything or blindly following the mind's orders. We don't follow all the advice we're given by sources outside ourselves. There's no reason we have to follow all the advice that comes from inside our mind.

When I was sitting in statistics class in graduate school one day, my mind told me to take off my black suede ankle boot and throw it through the window. Every day while I was in class, this thought came into my mind. At first, as any good student studying psychiatric diagnosis would do, I started to wonder if this was the beginning of a psychotic break. I could see it all: unzipping the boot, grasping it by its chunky yet well-cushioned heel, and chucking it through one of the high rectangular windows that lined one classroom wall. I could see my classmates and professor turning towards me in shock when they realized what I had done. All of this would of course be followed by my shameful expulsion from school, having had "unfit to be a psychologist" stamped across my forehead.

Dear reader, I did not chuck the boot through the window.

Not that day, and not any of the days that followed for the next three years. I eventually figured out that I didn't want to throw the boot (I was broke and these were my favorite shoes) and, more importantly, that I didn't have to throw the boot.

Because we don't have to do anything our mind says.

This may seem a little silly when we're talking about boots and windows, of course. More seriously, this realization likely saved my life a few times. You see, thoughts of suicide didn't stop after I left adolescence. They have been with me ever since, sometimes louder than others. They get very loud when I'm overwhelmed or severely sleep-deprived. My mind is trying to solve a problem, just in an extreme way. The best solution for being sleep-deprived is to try to go to bed and get some rest—ending it all just because I missed a couple of nights of sleep is a little extreme. But that's the mind for you. Minds tend to overreact. So my mind thinks of handy places to drive off high overpasses or other really bad ideas. I don't want to die. I actually like living and want to continue to do so. My mind just has the habit of offering suicide as the first option when it starts brainstorming. Therefore, when it brings up the idea, I respond by saying, "Nah, thanks for sharing, but I'd rather not. What else you got?" If I did believe what my mind was saying, then it would feel scary and miserable. It might even become dangerous if I decided to act on it. Since I don't believe my mind one bit when it gets going on this suicide spiel, I'm better able to let those thoughts just float by without acting on them.

The other gift of this approach is that there's less struggle. Less struggle to constantly monitor for "negative" thoughts and counter them. Less struggle to change thoughts. Less struggle to try to "think positive." The stream of thoughts can just run by us, and we can pull from it the things that seem useful, allowing the rest to move along.

I'm not saying that this is easy, not by a long shot. It takes practice and tools, which I'll give you more of soon. I am saying that, over time, shifting your relationship with your mind can help you live with more ease and freedom of movement. And you don't have to throw the boot.

EXPLORATIONS

What Have You Tried? Set a timer for 3 minutes and write down everything you've tried to make painful thoughts go away. Once the timer dings, read over the list. How successful have those efforts been at making the thoughts actually go away for good? What has been the cost of those attempts? (Be gentle with yourself here. We did the best we could with what we knew at the time. Remember, you're in the process of learning another way out of the cycles you've been stuck in for so long.)

Watching Thoughts: Sit for 3 minutes and watch your thoughts go by. You can imagine them as clouds moving across the sky, leaves floating down a stream, cars on a train that is passing by, billboards on the highway, or any other image that helps you experience the sensation of being able to watch your thoughts rather than be dragged along by them. There are many versions of this exercise available on YouTube and other places if you'd like a guided version. Do this mindfulness exercise once a day for a week. Notice when you're getting stuck to thoughts and when you are able to watch them. When you do notice that you're stuck to a thought and it's dragging you along, gently bring yourself back to the place of watching. Repeat a million times if necessary.

What are three things your mind tells you on a regular basis that feel really, really true? (You'll use these in the explorations for the next chapter.)

CHAPTER 7

Key Four: Doing the Unstuck

This brings us to the fourth key: Unsticking. Like Thanks But No Thanks, it can help give us more freedom to choose what we do, including freedom from beliefs we may have held for years or decades.

You know, this idea of thoughts flowing nicely by while we sit on the bank unaffected is a lovely picture. It'd make a nice painting, like something by Monet. In fact, it might as well be an Impressionistic painting, because it's not realistic.

There are moments, yes, of calm observation of the mind, of equanimity. It can happen more often with a steady mindfulness or meditation practice. When we see images of Buddhist monks meditating, I imagine that this is what they are doing—sitting calmly on the bank of the river and watching.

Especially at first, we more often end up stuck to some thought that drags us into the water and downstream for a bit, until we realize we've been caught and unstick ourselves. We climb, bedraggled and dripping, back onto the bank until the next sticky thought comes along. It doesn't have to be a "negative" thought either. It can be a daydream about the future or revising the grocery list. When I went to 6:30 a.m. Kundalini yoga classes, my mind spent a lot of the meditation time planning out what I was going to have for breakfast afterward.

Sticky thoughts are the ones that feel very real and very true. They're that infomercial offer we pick up the phone or hop online to buy, then wonder what on earth we were thinking when the package arrives. We don't question the authority of sticky thoughts or their source. Sometimes they seem like they must be fact simply because they come around so often or because they have an intense emotional impact. Perhaps they are echoes of what people in positions of authority (parents, teachers, friends, bosses) told us at some point.

We're stuck to a thought when we do Step 3 (We believe what our mind is saying) and start feeling and acting accordingly. There were examples of this in the previous chapter of being stuck to a thought about the headache and to a thought about depression. We can be stuck to a thought for years, even decades. It can become our guiding principle. Thoughts born of traumatic experiences, like "The world is completely unsafe" or "It was all my fault," can be especially sticky.

Being stuck to a thought isn't always negative, although even "positive" thoughts can impact our ability to be present and effective in our reactions to life events. If we get stuck to the thought that "I am a good person," it may be harder to continue to grow and to take in feedback about the areas in which we may be biased or unkind. Rose-colored glasses are still biased ones.

Our minds are not the enemy. When starting this work, it can be easy to fall into this type of thinking, which takes us back into the struggle we were just trying to leave. What I'm suggesting is to treat your mind like a well-intentioned but misguided friend. Perhaps it's a helicopter parent or a bored mall cop who's had five cans of Red Bull. For safety and survival purposes, we are wired to notice and remember the negative more than the positive. Our minds are just trying to help, but they're not equipped for the complexity of our modern lives that are so far removed from the binary simplicity of tiger or no tiger, live or die.

This is one of the ways to get unstuck—creating a persona for our minds. It could be simply "The Mind," or more elaborate, like a famous person, a fictional character, an animal, or something entirely imaginary. In my work with clients, I have seen minds personified as everything from Donald Duck to Rush Limbaugh. Another approach is to name aspects of our mind, such as calling the worrying part Anxious Sally or the angry defensive impulses The Guards. It can help to give our mind an image, a personality, even a voice. The sillier the better, as humor is a powerful unsticking agent. The goal here is to create something that you can start to develop a relationship with over time.

We can devise a phrase to use to politely blow off these thoughts. The important thing here is to first acknowledge them, since they'll get louder if we don't, and then thank them for their concern before turning your attention elsewhere. I like to tell my mind, "Thanks for sharing! I appreciate your concern," all in a just-barely-detectable sarcastic tone.

We can even label the sticky thoughts themselves. They often tend to travel in packs, so they can be a package deal. In my mind, these bundles get labels like the titles of episodes of *Friends*: "The One Where I'm a Hopeless Failure and Will Never Do Anything Right," or "The One Where I Should Just Give Up Already." These greatest hits are in syndication and love to rerun, so when I notice them, I tell myself, "ah, here we go again with this one—I know what happens in this episode," and try to just let it play itself out in the background without getting too caught up in it.

I'm not trying to say that these sticky thoughts aren't scary or upsetting sometimes. They can be downright terrifying, especially if the rerun is a traumatic memory or a panicky image of a disastrous future. What I want to convey is that thoughts are thoughts are thoughts. They are not reality. And we decide how much power we give them. We bestow that power through our belief. If we don't believe in them, if we don't feed them attention, they slide by just a little bit more easily. Like avoiding eye contact with someone handing out flyers on the sidewalk, just keep moving and they will fade into the background eventually, even if they follow us for half a block.

Another way to destroy some of the power of thoughts is to pull back the curtain and reveal the truth that they are merely sounds to which we have attributed meaning. They can feel so real and true. Think of a cookie. Any kind of cookie you want. Shape, size, texture, smell, taste--conjure it up in your mind as vividly as you can. Mouth watering yet?

Now set a timer and say the word "cookie" over and over as fast as you can for one minute. Yes, really. Cookiecookiecookiecookiecookiecookiecookiecookiecookiecookiecookie cookiecookiecookie.

What happened to the image of the cookie? Still there? Or has it changed somehow?

Exercises like this help us remember that words are just sounds. They are only as real as we believe they are. When we have a really sticky thought, or maybe a word that socks us in the gut, it can help to repeat it over and over like this for a minute or two to take some of the sting out of it. As you see above, writing it repeatedly (preferably by hand) can have a similar effect. Sounds goofy, I know. Remember, silliness and irreverence are powerful tools when dealing with our mind. Also, have the other things you've tried worked well for you? If so, what drew you to spend time reading this book? Play a little. Nothing to lose but your mind—I mean, your time.

EXPLORATIONS

If you haven't done it yet, do the cookiecookiecookie exercise in the chapter.

How do you know when you're stuck to a thought? What helps you get unstuck?

Casting: Create a persona for your mind. Give your mind a name and an image or character. It can be someone real or imaginary. It can even be multiple characters, such as a board of advisors, an entourage, or a rowdy family. Now find a way to remind yourself of that persona and put it somewhere you'll see it.

Cookie It! Those three things from the previous chapter's explorations that feel like they're really, really true? Cookie them! If they're short phrases, pick one, set your timer for a minute, and repeat it out loud as fast as you can over and over. If you're unable to speak, then write or sign it over and over and over, with no spaces between words. You can then do this process again with the other two phrases.

Title It: If one of those three things is a long story, then give it a title of some kind, the way episodes of TV shows are titled. Make it a little silly, like "The one where I'm a terrible failure and am going to destroy the world, blah blah blah."

Once you're done, just notice how you feel.

CHAPTER EIGHT

Key Five: Critters

We've talked a lot about thoughts thus far. They are important, but Key Five, Critters, brings us into the tricky and often mysterious realm of feelings, which many of us need a little extra help dealing with.

Perhaps one of the hardest things to figure out as a human with a mind is how to live with the critters we call emotions. Emotions themselves are little messengers. And they can be pretty darn good at getting us to spring into action (or stop everything).

Now, when I'm talking about emotions, I'm talking about the physical experience of an emotion in its raw form. I'm not talking about the meaning we give that experience, the stories that our mind tells us about it, or thoughts that are phrased using the word "feel" (i.e., I feel that we need to take the garbage out more often.)

Emotions have a distant relationship with words. Often we struggle to find the words to describe what we're feeling, and that makes sense, since we're trying to get the mind to describe something we are feeling within the body. However, simply naming an emotion can help tame it a little, wrap it into a package that we feel we can carry.

We've been given so many rules about emotions. That there's something wrong with us if we aren't feeling certain emotions (I'm looking at you, Happy) or if we are feeling other ones (yeah, I see you, Angry). That if we do experience an "unapproved" emotion, we need to DO SOMETHING about it right away, whether that be drown it in food or alcohol, take it out on someone else, dive into distractions, take a pill, bury ourselves in work, or just pull the covers over our head. We've been taught either to acquiesce to emotions and meet all their demands, or to completely wall them off and ignore them completely.

This makes emotions sound threatening indeed, like an invading army poised at our border who could start marching at any moment. When we live from this perspective, we are ever-vigilant, scrambling to see what we can do to keep them quiet or shoo them away.

But when was the last time we actually stopped and looked an emotion square in the eye? Asked it what it wanted to tell us? Got curious? Yes, curiosity is back again to save the day.

Here's when I learned the power of curiosity. Sometime around 2008, I was encouraged...well, more like nearly coerced, to attend a self-care retreat for mental health providers. I dragged my feet all the way there. Right before leaving town, I had been diagnosed with fibromyalgia and spondylolisthesis (a mouthful of vowels meaning two vertebrae in the spine that are out of alignment), plus there was a cyst in my spine that made my left side numb every time I twisted my torso or did a backbend. This news sent me swirling in spirals of grief about what I could no longer physically do, especially my favorite yoga poses. Before the appointment, I had been thinking of taking up running, and now I was told that was also a no-go. Not to mention that I had pain all over my body, the kind of pain that comes with the flu, when even your hair aches. The last thing I wanted to do at this point was be present with anything or anyone. I just wanted to pull on my way-oversized navy blue sweatpants, grab a light British romance from my pile of crinkly-covered library books, and curl up on the couch with some popcorn like I did every day.

This retreat had other plans for me. There are more stories of how it wiggled in and started sparks inside my blah self, but just one will do for now. We had the option to go to a morning meditation, which I dragged myself to just like I dragged myself to everything else. The second day, on that hard lumpy cushion with both me and my leg half-asleep, after about ten minutes of wondering what breakfast would be that day, I had little cartoonish characters appear in my mind. One was a Pepto-Bismol pink, spiky, squishy round thing; the other an animate version of the toy that has a dog's head and tail connected by a Slinky. I knew right away they were named Fibro and Spondy. Weirdly enough, instead of being more sucked into the grief and misery of the pain and loss, I was chuckling to myself. My breath came a little easier. And I carry them with me to this day, affectionately.

So what the heck happened on that cushion? Why was I chuckling at something that had been making me so miserable?

I could do that because I had found a way to have a relationship with my sensations. Giving them an image and personalities meant that I could now interact with them instead of being caught in a power struggle with an overwhelming abstract concept. Plus, now that I could look at them, they were even kind of cute. And the more I sat with these images, the more I noticed that they would fluctuate— sometimes grow, sometimes shrink, sometimes go quiet, sometimes scream. The pain was always there, but it wasn't always the same. I could start to appreciate the moments when it eased and remind myself that the intense moments would fade.

Later, when I trained in ACT, I found out that this thing I did on accident is an actual technique that I can teach clients. And I'm happy to teach it to you too.

As with any new skill, it's best to start with something small, just until we get the hang of the steps involved. At first, try this out when you're feeling relatively calm, not when in the midst of a panic attack.

1) To start, sit comfortably, letting the spine be long and tall without straining. Let out a long exhale.

2) Using your attention like a scanner, look though your body to see what physical sensations catch your attention, selecting one to be your focus. The sensation you pick can be pleasant or unpleasant, doesn't matter.

3) Once you select a sensation to be your focus, imagine you're pulling it out from its spot in your body so that you can observe it more closely. Let it float in the air in front of you. Now get curious. What does it look like? How big is it? What color(s)? Texture(s)? Temperature? Does it move or is it stationary? Does it make a sound or have something to say? Anything else you notice with your senses?

Note: The mind will really really REALLY want to tell a story about what all this means and worry about why this sensation is present and how long it will stay and what it says about you that you're having it, etc. See if you can let the mind's commentary be background noise and refocus on your senses. Refocus as many times as you need to.

4) Sit, breathe, and watch this critter for a moment. See if you can allow it to be there. Remember that no matter how big and scary it may appear, it can't actually harm you. You can choose in any moment to open your eyes and distract yourself if you need to. Remind yourself that you have experienced many, many big emotions and sensations in the past, and you survived them all.

5) As you watch the critter, scan your body again and see if any other sensations catch your attention. If so, choose one to pull out and observe it as a second critter, letting it hang in the air next to the first one. Sit, breathe, and observe it with all the senses, remembering to refocus when you notice you're caught up in the mind's chatter.

6) Repeat the process one more time with a third critter if desired.

7) Here's the big one. With willingness, scoop up the critters and allow them to return to their spots. Remember that they are already there anyway, so you know you can handle welcoming them in. Long exhale, noticing how that feels. Critters may or may not have shifted during flight, and that's okay.

The key here is not to try to make anything go away, although sometimes we may notice that emotions or sensations shrink or change during the process of watching them. What we gain through an exercise like this is the ability to sit in the midst of an emotion or sensation and not feel compelled to do anything to make it go away. If we can manage to do this, with practice we learn that we don't have to immediately jump to a solution for an emotion. We learn that we can look an emotion in the eye and not have to run from it or bow to its every command. This, dear ones, is freedom. It can open a door to freedom from compulsions, from addictions, from being held prisoner by fear or anxiety. It's another superpower, especially when we combine it with the ability to not do everything our mind says.

Here's an easy way to remember the process:

W: Where is it? Scan to determine where the emotion or sensation is located in your body

O: Objectively observe the critter, using all your senses

E: Expand, willingly welcoming the critter(s), knowing you have room for this feeling and many more

EXPLORATIONS

What have you been told about feelings throughout your life? What messages did you get about how to cope with feelings?

What feeling is the most challenging for you? Which feeling is the least challenging?

What feeling seems like it holds you back the most from doing what you want to do?

WOE It: Try out the WOE technique at least three times this week. Remember that you can use it on physical sensations as well as emotions. Start small so that you can learn the technique first before moving on to the more challenging emotions. Notice what comes up for you. When you feel overwhelmed, remember, you're the sky, not the clouds.

CHAPTER NINE

Key Six: What Do You Mean?

Really, what do you mean? What is the meaning of your time here on the planet? What is important to you?

I'm asking this because the answers to these questions are where our energy lies. We often talk about not feeling motivated. Meaning is the key to motivation. If something isn't connected to something that's important to us, we're naturally not going to want to do it.

There are a few levels of this motivation and choice stuff. One is composed of the things that feel important because they are related to survival. They're not all that fun sometimes, but we do them anyway. Such situations usually include some element of time pressure and undesirable and immediate consequences. I think of this every time I go camping and finally find a cosy position to sleep in, nestled in my sleeping bag that has reached an ideal temperature while the air grows cooler and cooler outside. Then I have to pee. My mind can't get me out of that pickle, no matter how much I deny it and try to bargain with my bladder. There is nothing to be done but choose if I am to wet my sleeping bag and clothes or if I am to climb out, fumble for the tent zipper, slip on shoes damp with dew, and stumble to wherever the appropriate spot may be.

As with so much of this mind stuff, the farther we get from nature, the more complex it becomes, and the easier it is to say no or delay deciding. This level includes things like creating something, taking an emotional risk, changing careers, telling the truth to someone, lifting weights, or writing a book. We can spend decades deciding what we want to do. We can spend even longer deciding how we want to do it. And we can spend a lifetime waiting for the motivation to show up.

Motivation is not required for action. We don't have to feel like doing something to be able to do the action. Believe me, the last thing I feel like doing is getting up out of my warm sleeping bag to go pee. And yet I do it. I didn't feel like sitting here and writing this sentence today. And I did it, and wrote a few more after that to boot. I did it because it was important to me to try to help others with what I have learned.

Meaning is what makes it easier to take action. No matter what we are doing, if we can link it to something that is important to us, there's more energy behind it. At the beginning of yoga classes there is often an invitation to set an intention for this very reason.

Please note that I am not here to tell you *what* should be important to you. This is completely up to you. It can be challenging to sort out what we have been told should matter to us from what actually does matter to us. But this is your life and you get to decide. You also get to change your mind at any point and revise the whole shebang. (I know, ack! Choices! Eek!)

We get to choose what we want our lives to be about, what qualities we want to embody. Choosing may not be as hard as your mind is saying it will be, since you have been alive for some time now (I am assuming) and have likely formed some opinions about things. Here are some guidelines when considering this:

Where's the focus? When choosing qualities, make sure that they are things that we can control--we don't get much say in the behavior and choices of others. Instead, we need to focus on how we want to be in the world. For example, we could say that we want to be a parent to five children, but we don't have complete say in whether or not that happens. Instead, we could say that we want to be nurturing to others. See how that works? Same concept, but more general and more under our control. Even if we don't have children, we could find many ways to be nurturing.

Is it infinite? When talking qualities, we're talking about things that we can never completely achieve. It's not like we are honest once and *check* we've officially reached "honest person status." These qualities are like the cardinal directions; they give us a general orientation but we never really get there. Say we're in Texas and we want to go east. We can have many stops along the way, like New Orleans, the Atlantic Ocean, India, but we'll never actually reach East, just like we'll never actually reach Honest.

Is it important enough? Is this something that fires you up, that you want people to use to describe you after you're gone, that you'd feel like you lived well if someone said this about you in an award speech? Is this something you'd like to see more of in the world? That you'd inscribe on your crest if you were a medieval knight? We're talking about qualities that are our guiding lights here—they have to light us up inside.

Is it yours? As I mentioned earlier, we can get really tangled up in what our families and societies taught us about what should be meaningful to us. If need be, make two lists of qualities: one of the ones you think should be important to you and one of the qualities that actually are important to you.

This may seem like yet another silly exercise in yet another self-help book. Just humor me here. This is key to doing the other things. I promise. We're talking the meaning of life here—well, the meaning of your life. What's more important than that?

EXPLORATIONS

Take a little time and list qualities that are coming to mind as you read this chapter. You can sort through them later. If you're stuck, think of various areas of your life: What kind of family member do you want to be? What kind of employee/employer? What is important to you in the areas of health, leisure, community, spirituality?

Create Your Compass: Once you have your list, see which five qualities stand out to you the most. Some may overlap, so choose the one that seems to best sum up what you want to embody. These are your compass points. Try them on mentally and see how it feels in your body when you think of taking actions that are in line with these qualities. Imagine using them to guide your choices. If it doesn't sit right with you, revise the list and try it on again. Do this until you have a list that fits you like your favorite comfy clothes.

Try It On: Now that you've found your five qualities, pick one each day and let it be your intention for that day. For example, if you pick kindness, then see how kindly you can do everything you do that day. You can answer the phone kindly, feed the dog kindly, sit kindly, breathe kindly. You don't have to change what you do, just how you do it. When you lie down in bed at the end of the day, review what you did and notice how it feels to have your actions line up with what's most important to you. They can't always line up perfectly, but having them do so more often than not can feel really good.

CHAPTER TEN

Key Seven: Running Experiments

We've been talking a lot about not believing everything our mind says, as well as ways to do this by getting unstuck from our thoughts and feelings. This is an internal approach to creating shifts in our lives.

As I mentioned before, there comes a point when external action is needed as well. We can work from the outside in, trying out new ways of doing things and testing our mind's theories. Most importantly, we then need to notice the result in a mindful manner.

Experiments can be all kinds of things. Here are steps you can follow to design your next experiment (insert your best mad scientist cackle here if you like):

1. *Identify a theory that you'd like to test.* This theory can be based on past experiences (that one time that you spilled food on yourself at that one party 10 years ago) or things that your mind has told you (if you go to that event, you'll make a fool of yourself).

2. *Select a way to test that theory.* There can be multiple tests over time—start with what feels manageable. Sticking with the above example, this could be going to a small social

event with only close friends, or going to a larger one and staying for a short time. It could even start with having a conversation with someone in line at the store. Just make sure that it is something that really matters to you. If you hate baseball and never have a need to go to a baseball game in your life and no one you know plays baseball, then don't go to a baseball game. On the other hand, if your sister's child or your grandchild plays baseball and you want to support them, then being able to go to baseball games might become very important. Everyone is different.

3. *Record your results.* Physically recording them somewhere is best, since it will give you a document you can refer back to when psyching yourself up to run the next experiment. If you can't write them down or record yourself describing them, call or text a friend (or therapist) and tell them about it.

4. *Focus on what you can control.* We can't always predict or create a certain outcome. That's okay. Even if the situation didn't go the way you hoped, there are ways that you can succeed on a personal level. Did you act in a way that was in line with what is important to you? Did you do what you could? Remember, even running the experiment meant that you displayed courage and willingness to be more free.

5. *Feelings are not failures.* Maybe you felt anxious, perhaps even to the point of having a panic attack. Maybe you felt shaky and sweaty. None of that detracts from your courage and accomplishment. Don't rate your success on how you felt. If anything, you get bonus points for feeling all of that and doing it anyway!

6. *Pause to acknowledge what you were able to do and your willingness to stretch yourself.* Rewards can be very nice

at this point and can be anything from a cosy night in to a material object.

7. *Review what you learned and plan the next experiment.* Repeat as many times as needed on as many theories as needed. (Hint: this is a lifelong process.)

EXPLORATIONS

You guessed it--your exploration for this week is to run experiments! Pick three experiments you want to run, following the seven steps in this chapter.

Record your results:
    What did you set out to do?

    Did you do it?

    If you didn't, what sticky thoughts, feelings, or circumstances felt like they got in the way?

    If you did do it, what thoughts and feelings did you have to be willing to feel in order to do it? How did you find a way to do your experiment anyway?

    How did you reward yourself?

What's the next step (if any)?

CHAPTER ELEVEN

Key Eight: The Most Important Question

Here's what it all comes down to. We've talked about noticing. We've explored what is meaningful to you. We've put the mind in its place and learned how to shake loose from those sticky thoughts. We've remembered that our essence is vast and indestructible.

Knowing all that, here's the big question. Here, I'll even write it so that it's big. Because it's that big.

Are you willing?

Willingness is about being open, being available. To be willing, we don't have to know how yet. We just have to be ready to take an action and see what happens, hands open, shoulders relaxed and down. This is different than willfulness, which is our arms crossed across our chest, chin stubborn, determined to control our experience and anything else we can get our hands on.

In fact, let's try that on in our bodies right now. First, let's adopt a willful stance (great time to channel your inner rebellious teenager) and see how that feels. How does our breathing change? Our body feel? Now, open that up into a more willing stance and notice changes, if any, in breath and body. When I'm in session with clients or in a conversation in my personal life, I am mindful of my hands and try to keep them as open as possible, reopening them if I notice them wanting to ball up and clench. It's a helpful visual and physical reminder to stay open and willing.

Willingness says, "let's talk about it" and "let's see." Willfulness says, "only on my terms" and "prove it to me first."

Willfulness arises when we're fighting reality and refusing to acknowledge it. Physically, it feels like bracing ourselves for impact. Hackles are up, muscles are tense.

Willingness is still strong, but with a softness, a more permeable membrane. Willingness allows reality in just as it is.

Willingness is not being a doormat or being passive. It is simply a stance. It's a starting point from which we can move however we see fit, often more effectively since we're able to work with reality. When we're willing, it also takes less energy to act since we're not devoting attention and resources to willfulness.

We'll dip in and out of willingness throughout our lives, depending on the situation and other factors. Our levels of willingness will change too. All of that is perfectly fine. Even being willing some of the time is a shift, so start small. See where it is possible to open to the reality of this experience.

This leads to the Big Question in its full form: What are we willing to feel and experience in order to do the things that are important to us and that will help us move in the direction of a life that feels satisfying and worthwhile?

EXPLORATIONS

Here's the Big Question again:

What are we willing to feel and experience in order to do the things that are important to us and that will help us move in the direction of a life that feels satisfying and worthwhile?

Let's break it down so you can answer it piece by piece, pulling together everything you've learned thus far on your journey:

What are you willing to feel and experience? What have you learned that can help you be more willing?

What are the things that are important to you? What qualities do you want to embody?

What does a life that feels satisfying and worthwhile look like for you? If you were at your 100th birthday party looking back on your life, how would you want to say that you lived it?

Lastly, in the next week, what three steps can you take towards making that image a reality?

My Love Note to All of Us

My fellow human beans,

Life is hard stuff. It really is. It's not anything that you did wrong. It's just hard! It's constant work and struggle, and pain is frequent.

It's also gorgeous at times. Those times slip by us because we're not naturally geared to notice them. Pleasure and enjoyment are not key to surviving being attacked by lions, so our system overlooks them. We have to savor them intentionally and repeatedly for them to stick.

You may get sold a fairy-tale idea that it will be all be better when this or that thing happens. Don't buy it. It's flimsy as a plastic tiara. It's better now. Your life is happening now. Cheesy, cheesy, I know, but it's for real. Like right now, folks.

So please, just for me if not for yourself, take a moment and look around today. See what new thing you can notice as you walk out your door. Take five seconds to really taste that first sip of your morning beverage. Hug a loved one just a second longer. Bring yourself into your life.

If you practice this, you may find that so much of what you long for is already here. We might feel restless and crave novelty when the reality is that things are changing all the time, even inside our own bodies. We might crave elaborate luxury and indulgent lifestyles, when there is just as much luxury in the last notes of a piece of dark chocolate melting on the tongue, in socks warm from the dryer on a cold morning, in a burst of colorful wildflowers on the road near the bus stop.

Let your attention and your intention be powerful tools with which to nourish yourself. Be willing and open to receiving all the gifts in your life in these moments. Maybe once we're well-fed, we'll be more open and compassionate towards the other residents of this planet. It can start with you. And it can start now.

I'm so honored to have spent this time with you. Thank you. Remember, none of this is selfish. When you're happier and healthier, we're all happier and healthier.

May you not only build a satisfying life for yourself but also allow yourself to notice and enjoy it.

Love,

Dr. Jo

Acknowledgments

Gratitude is one of my favorite practices. None of this would be possible without the following, in no particular order:

My clients and students, for all that they have taught me over the years.

My own therapists, guides, and yoga teachers for your patience with my squirmy struggles. The ACT community, including the people on the listserv whose faces I've never seen. Miss Herring, my fifth-grade teacher who was the first teacher to encourage my writing. The Coming Home Project for creating the provider retreat where Spondy and Fibro showed up.

My dear friends in the Enterprise Resonance group who read drafts and kept me accountable, and Bhadra for copyediting. The women whose companionable silence at our monthly retreat created space for so much of this book to be written.

Amrit at Sage House for cover design and patience, Hayley for your belief in this book, and Sohan for all the encouragement and pictures of vintage toasters. David for saving me with his computer whispering.

My mother for passing along her love of language to me.

My father and brother and the rest of the Eckler clan for being understanding when I disappeared for long stretches of time to work on this book. I love you all so much.

My (actual) critter companions who barked and purred and snored through rewrites and edits.

And in a very special place, my beloved partner Jack for his endless support and patience. I adore you, darlin' darling.

ABOUT THE AUTHOR

Dr. Jo Eckler procrastinates writing by working as a licensed clinical psychologist and registered yoga teacher in Austin, TX. Her mission is to help others find more self-compassion, meaning, and conscious choice in their lives. Learn more at www.beyondtherapy.us

About the Publisher

Spiral Staircase Publishing got its name from a strong belief that healing is like walking up a spiral staircase. Sometimes we get tired, sometimes it seems daunting, and sometimes we'd rather just sit for a while. It can also feel like we are going in circles and not getting anywhere. However, each time we circle around, we have moved up a little higher, we have learned a little more, and we have a little more breathing space from the initial hurt. Let's all keep walking, together, up towards the light. Wherever you are on your journey, we hope our books offer you encouragement, humor, and support along the way.

Printed in Australia
AUHW011909150120
322451AU00032B/76